POOL
(NO WATER)

by Mark Ravenhill

‖SAMUEL FRENCH‖

samuelfrench.co.uk

Copyright © 2006 by Mark Ravenhill
All Rights Reserved

POOL (NO WATER) is fully protected under the copyright laws of the British Commonwealth, including Canada, the United States of America, and all other countries of the Copyright Union. All rights, including professional and amateur stage productions, recitation, lecturing, public reading, motion picture, radio broadcasting, television and the rights of translation into foreign languages are strictly reserved.

ISBN 978-0-573-11611-7

www.samuelfrench.co.uk
www.samuelfrench.com

FOR AMATEUR PRODUCTION ENQUIRIES

UNITED KINGDOM AND WORLD
EXCLUDING NORTH AMERICA
plays@samuelfrench.co.uk
020 7255 4302/01

Each title is subject to availability from Samuel French,
depending upon country of performance.

CAUTION: Professional and amateur producers are hereby warned that *POOL (NO WATER)* is subject to a licensing fee. Publication of this play does not imply availability for performance. Both amateurs and professionals considering a production are strongly advised to apply to the appropriate agent before starting rehearsals, advertising, or booking a theatre. A licensing fee must be paid whether the title is presented for charity or gain and whether or not admission is charged.

The professional rights in this play are controlled by Judy Daish Associates Ltd, 2 St Charles Pl, London W10 6EG.

No one shall make any changes in this title for the purpose of production. No part of this book may be reproduced, stored in a retrieval system, or transmitted in any form, by any means, now known or yet to be invented, including mechanical, electronic, photocopying, recording, videotaping, or otherwise, without the prior written permission of the publisher. No one shall upload this title, or part of this title, to any social media websites.

The right of Mark Ravenhill to be identified as author of this work has been asserted in accordance with Section 77 of the Copyright, Designs and Patents Act 1988.

THINKING ABOUT PERFORMING A SHOW?

There are thousands of plays and musicals available to perform from Samuel French right now, and applying for a licence is easier and more affordable than you might think

From classic plays to brand new musicals, from monologues to epic dramas, there are shows for everyone.

Plays and musicals are protected by copyright law, so if you want to perform them, the first thing you'll need is a licence. This simple process helps support the playwright by ensuring they get paid for their work and means that you'll have the documents you need to stage the show in public.

Not all our shows are available to perform all the time, so it's important to check and apply for a licence before you start rehearsals or commit to doing the show.

LEARN MORE & FIND THOUSANDS OF SHOWS

Browse our full range of plays and musicals, and find out more about how to license a show

www.samuelfrench.co.uk/perform

Talk to the friendly experts in our Licensing team for advice on choosing a show and help with licensing

plays@samuelfrench.co.uk   020 7387 9373

Acting Editions

BORN TO PERFORM

Playscripts designed from the ground up to work the way you do in rehearsal, performance and study

---

Larger, clearer text for easier reading

Wider margins for notes

Performance features such as character and props lists, sound and lighting cues, and more

---

+ CHOOSE A SIZE AND STYLE TO SUIT YOU

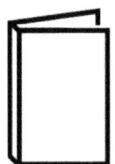

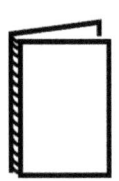

STANDARD EDITION	**SPIRAL-BOUND EDITION**	**LARGE EDITION**
Our regular paperback book at our regular size	The same size as the Standard Edition, but with a sturdy, easy-to-fold, easy-to-hold spiral-bound spine	A4 size and spiral bound, with larger text and a blank page for notes opposite every page of text – perfect for technical and directing use

| LEARN MORE | samuelfrench.co.uk/actingeditions

MUSIC USE NOTE

Licensees are solely responsible for obtaining formal written permission from copyright owners to use copyrighted music in the performance of this play and are strongly cautioned to do so. If no such permission is obtained by the licensee, then the licensee must use only original music that the licensee owns and controls. Licensees are solely responsible and liable for all music clearances and shall indemnify the copyright owners of the play(s) and their licensing agent, Samuel French, against any costs, expenses, losses and liabilities arising from the use of music by licensees. Please contact the appropriate music licensing authority in your territory for the rights to any incidental music.

IMPORTANT BILLING AND CREDIT REQUIREMENTS

If you have obtained performance rights to this title, please refer to your licensing agreement for important billing and credit requirements.

**Other plays by MARK RAVENHILL
published and licensed by Samuel French**

Candide

Citizenship

Ghost Story

Golden Child

Handbag

Mother Clap's Molly House

Over There

Product

Scenes from Family Life

Shoot/Get Treasure/Repeat

Shopping and Fucking

Some Explicit Polaroids

The Cut

The Experiment

**FIND PERFECT PLAYS TO PERFORM AT
www.samuelfrench.co.uk/perform**

ABOUT THE AUTHOR

Mark Ravenhill was born in Haywards Heath, West Sussex in 1966. He studied Drama and English at Bristol University. His first play *Shopping and Fucking* was produced by Out of Joint and the Royal Court Theatre in 1996. Subsequent plays include *Faust Is Dead* and *Handbag* (both Actors Touring Company), *Some Explicit Polaroids* (Out of Joint at the Ambassadors Theatre), *Mother Clap's Molly House* and *Citizenship* (both National Theatre), *Pool (No Water)* (Frantic Assembly at the Lyric Theatre), *The Cut* (Donmar Theatre), *Shoot/Get Treasure/ Repeat* (Paines Plough) and *Over There* (Royal Court). From 2012 to 2014, Mark was playwright in residence for the Royal Shakespeare Company, producing a new version of Brecht's *Galileo* and a new play *Candide* inspired by Voltaire (both Swan Theatre, Stratford-Upon-Avon). Mark's work in music theatre includes a new English version of Monteverdi's *The Coronation of Poppea* with additional material by Michael Nyman (King's Head); *Ten Plagues*, a song cycle for Marc Almond with composer Connor Mitchell (Traverse Theatre) and *Elysium* with composer Rolf Wallin for the Norwegian Opera. Mark is the co-creator of the ITV sitcom *Vicious*.

A Frantic Assembly, Drum Theatre Plymouth and Lyric Hammersmith Production, *Pool (No Water)* was first performed at the Drum Theatre Plymouth on 22 September 2006.

The cast was as follows:

Keir Charles
Cait Davis
Leah Muller
Mark Rice-Oxley

Directed and choreographed by	Scott Graham and Steven Hoggett
Designed by	Miriam Buether
Lighting design by	Natasha Chivers
Music by	Imogen Heap

The original production had four speakers – A, B, C, D. Other productions don't have to follow this.

A pool, she had a pool.

Of all of us the most – at least in the eyes of this so-called world – the most successful of us.

So – a pool.

Did she mean to impress? Was it for show?

No. I can't think. No. Because she's...

She's good. She's nice. She has integrity. Her roots.

And she has a pool now – it's fantastic fantastic fantastic fantastic.

But she hasn't forgotten us. Visits to rehab. Visits to hospices. Visits to Aids wards. She's made them.

And she comes to our exhibitions. Cramped little exhibitions in lofts in the bohemian quarter. Our photos, our *objets trouvés,* she comes, she sees, she sometimes buys. And she'll help our fundraising drives.

She's tireless in her help for our fund-raising drives.

We adore her. We adore her. We all absolutely adore her.

Years ago when she was in – when she was in the Group. Life and soul. And she'd always be ripping her clothes off, just ripping them off, and we'd all rip them off too – we'd follow her – and then we'd all make performance pieces or art-house shorts or we'd just go skinny-dipping for the sheer naked fun of it.

But nowadays she's...absent.

Exactly. She's...absent. It's that quality in her work that sells. The pieces that first began when we lost Ray to the whole Aids thing. And she used Ray's blood and bandages and catheter and condoms. Pieces that sold to every major collector in the world.

Aha.

Absent. And yet somehow – recognised by the world.

Aha.

And now she has: the pool. The poooooooooool.

First seen in attachments. A Christmas attachment. Open the attachment for a PDF of my new pool.

I open with caution. I have a fear of viruses.

Her pool. "You're welcome at any time. Come over, share the pool. Any of you – singularly or together – just come over and enjoy the pool."

And there's the PDF. There's the pool. Clean and blue and lit by beautiful lights. And there's the pool boy – who could have been a porn star. Or maybe is a porn star. Or will be a porn star. And there's her personal trainer taking her through her lengths. And he's a porn star too. And maybe the pool boy fucks the trainer. Or the trainer fucks her. Or she fucks the pool boy.

No no no no – she's always been a very moral person. She's always had a strict code of morals. Even in the hovel days. She never did the hah-hah-heroin for more than a day. And she always kept her door strictly shut at night.

And so we email each other back and forth: Yes, let's go and see the pool, let's go and share the pool, why not? Why not? Let's share it with her.

And we email her back. We're coming, we're coming, we're all coming. We're all getting on a plane and coming over to share the pool with you.

And she Es back: Fantastic. Fantastic. Fantastic.

Time drifts, of course. We're all busy – there's exhibitions in the bohemian quarter, there's a project to provide murals for heroin babies, there's fundraising, there's—

There's Sally in the hospice. Sally in that fucking hospice. It's got into her bones now, it's eaten through her body and now that little evil cunting C is eating into her bones – it's got a taste of marrow – and she lies there and she says:

I want to die I want to die all I want is to die why can't they just let I won't take the medication when all I want is to die?

And we say to her:

Think of the pool. Think of the pool. That's something to keep going for. We'll get you out of here and fly you out to the pool. Fantastic healing healthy happy times ahead at the pool.

And she says:

Yes.

But that's just to humour us. Nobody believes that.

And Sally turns green and Sally turns grey and there's a drip drip drip stuck everywhere and nurses and nuns and we organise a rota because life must go on with its exhibitions and its fund-raising and we take it in turns until we all rush there one night and some of us make it and some of us don't and that's Sally done for.

And you're just stripped naked because suddenly all the art was worth nothing, it is nothing, it means nothing. Sally has gone and Art did nothing and Art could do nothing and Death is big and we are small and really we're nothing, we're nothing.

And *she's* there at the crematorium. And she says: "Thank you for looking after Sally. Thank you for that. You were all amazing for looking after. I'm so guilty. I should have been here sooner." And we're: No no no no no.

But I felt did you feel, listen I felt, this is wrong I know this is wrong but I felt, maybe it's only – did anyone else feel – and it is only a feeling, but a feeling is a feeling and I think that should be honoured, you know? If you know what I'm saying? Okay, okay, I'm going to say it, I'm going to tell you, I'm going to tell you what I what I felt, standing in the crematorium and suddenly she's there with her manager or whoever the, she's there and I want to scream at her: Cunt.

God.

Yes, just open my lungs and scream at her: "Cunt. Cunt –
this is your doing. You did this. You see this casket? You see
this casket, see this cheap horrible wooden casket with our
friend Sally in it? You did that. That was you."

God.

"It was you who killed Sally."

God.

"Because none of us was meant to be wealthy, none of us
was meant to be recognised, none of us was meant to fly.
We're the Group. And there's balance. And you took away
the balance. One of us goes up, then one of us goes down.
It's a natural law. Don't you understand the most basic
natural law? Well of course you do – understood it and
ignored it – on purpose – and killed Sally. Chose to kill
Sally. Cunt. Cunt. Cunt." And if I could I would have torn
her hair from her head and torn the clothes from her body
and spat into her cunt right then and right there; that was
what I... Did anyone else...?

No no no no one else. I see. I see. I see.

You see, what bad people. We are all bad people. It needn't
be that way of course. No. It needn't. If only we'd use our
Art for some good. But instead we harbour...

And I think maybe have always harboured, you know right
since the hovel, harboured...

Now we reflect...

Isn't that strange? All the time she was amongst us as a
friend, all that time and yet really we harboured the most
awful...well I suppose *hatred*.

Murderous hatred

Would be the only word.

Well that's awful. That is truly terrible.

Yes it is – and we must let that go. We must. Both with our
work with the heroin babies, but also in our attitude to her.
We must embrace her. We must love her. We must move

forward and let go of the past and let go of the badness and move forward with our love for her.

"You're all wiped out," she says. "You're all exhausted," she says. "Physically and spiritually and emotion. Please come out to the pool. Please. Please. Come on. It's the least I can do."

And so we all say: Yes.

Oh let's leave hatred let's leave death let's leave that behind. The poooooool.

And we go.

It takes so many hours to fly to this strange new world and there are palm trees and heat haze in the dusk of the airport.

And she's there:

Welcome welcome welcome.

And in the huge hallway of the house there's the pool boy and the personal trainer and the cook:

Hello. Hey. Hi. Welcome. Good to. Yeah. How ya? Come on make yourselves anything I can? Fantastic. So you're? Heard so much. That's good.

And yes – we feel a little guilty when we think of all the suffering back in the city – the beatings and the orphan and the pain – and for a moment we want to rush back there and make some art. But we take a moment, take a moment to let that pass – because really are we responsible for every baby whose mother is a junkie? That would be vanity.

And we look at her and we see... Yes, really you're just a person. A person like us. And – why did we feel those terrible things all these years? Oh it feels good to have let them go. And we notice how graceful her movements are and how beautiful her laugh sounds and we actually rather adore the way she's not so present – so pushing herself at you – so *there* as other people are.

And we each of us hold her and say: "It's good to be here. It's great to see you." And we actually mean it. And we are lighter than we have been for years.

You know she's a marvellous person. One of us, out in the world and doing well. It's time to celebrate that.

And that night there's a meal – swordfish and watercress and cool cool wine and we get reminiscent and we get cosy and we get tearful. About the – God, do you remember when we are all together when it all seemed to mean so much when everything was so full of meaning yes it was all drenched in meaning and we all cared we all cared so so passionately? Do you remember do you remember do you remember do you remember do you remember the days? Ah yes happy happy happy happy happy happy happy happy days.

I remember...very bright colours. In the crib. In the school. In that first studio we shared. I remember everything having so much colour that I felt: "God, how can I ever find a medium that has so much colour?"

Time for bed.

And each of us is in a bed.

But suddenly she's there, suddenly her head is round the door:

"I know we said sleep but I thought skinny-dipping let's come on skinny-dipping in the pool before bed."

God she hasn't lost it despite everything despite all this grandeur she's still...naughty naughty naughty.

Magic words from long ago: sk-iii-nn-eeee-dippp-pinnnggg. And we're back out into the night and we're giggling and we're drunk and there's no light in the grounds there's no light on the pool everything's been switched off. And we say: Clothes off. Because isn't that the naughtiest, most alive, most wonderful...? Clothes off.

And we take off our clothes.

And each of us knows that our body is not what it was those ten years before – that there's sag and fat and lines even and even even the littlest hints of grey. Oh yes the sad sad rot to the grave has already begun.

But that doesn't matter in the darkness. In the darkness we're as we were ten years ago when we strip poker and performance pieces and all that naked fun.

And it's just so beautiful. Slightest breeze around your cracks, hanging a little in the wind.

And some of us cry and some of us laugh but we're all moved by the sheer naked beauty of it.

I'll always remember that moment, always. Just something... all of us standing there naked in the dark. Sometimes now when the painkillers aren't working I try to visualise that moment and then things don't seem so awful.

Come on she squeals come on the pool!

And then she's running and whooping through the darkness and she launches herself and you can just see her up in the sky, up against the sky, the arc of her body through the night sky up and up and up and up.

She seems so high. She's flying. She's an angel. A drunken laughing goddess angel.

And then she arcs down and we're clapping and we're cheering.

And then

Some of us thought we heard the splash. You do. When you think there's going to be a splash then you hear a splash. You do the work. But we didn't hear the splash. There was no splash. There was

The crack

The cracking of her body.

The harsh crack of her body against the concrete.

Then there was silence.

Then there was her groan and her squeal and her screams of pain.

Aaaaaaggghoooowoooooowooowwwwwwww.

We edge forward in the darkness our naked figures moving forward in the dark until we're at the edge at the pool. And then we see, see as our eyes adjust

Pool. No water.

Just hints of water in a pool now drained.

And there in the middle of the concrete her body twisted and crunched and crushed and her noise now animal no more of god or angel. Ooooaaaaaawwwww.

We don't speak. We don't look at each other. We're too together now to need to look or speak to each other at all.

And we climb down and we climb down into the pool.

And we stand around her.

She was still conscious then. Still screaming and crying and jerking.

And we wanted to feel what she was feeling – she is one of us, we are artists – no, we're people – we wanted to feel what she was feeling – share the pain.

But it didn't happen.

We stood. We stood and we watched the jerking and we heard the screams. And we stood and we watched. All of us.

We couldn't do anything. Couldn't touch her. But we could have felt something. A life without empathy is...

She didn't jerk for long. She...went. Did she die? I suppose for a moment it crossed my mind and I was – no she didn't die and I think somehow we knew she didn't die. She "passed from consciousness".

And the great absent thing is lying at our feet and we're thinking:

"This is right. This feels – there is right in that."

I'm sorry you had to suffer, I'm sorry there's this pain – but there is justice in this. Something is shaping our ends.

For Sally, for Ray, for us, this had to be.

You see you flew – yes – you reached out your wings and you flew above us. And that's okay. You tried and congratulations. For trying. But you thought that could last? Flying above the ground, looking down on our lives in the city below? You really thought that could last? Of course that couldn't last. And now you've crashed right down. And that hurts doesn't it? I understand. That hurts.

This feels good. This feels wonderful. Look at you. Hah. Hah. Just look at you. I am great.

There is strength in me. Oh the strength in me I never knew I had.

You bitch you bitch you bitch you bitch you bitch you bitch you bitch.

And we

Maybe you will die. Maybe death will come for you. And if it's come for you, it hasn't come for me. That's me saved for another day.

And we

You shit you shit you evil evil evil evil shit to think these things of another person what kind of evil lies inside you?

And we

You've patronised my. You've patronised my exhibitions in the bohemian quarter. At last at last I can patronise you. I can care. What better way to patronise you back than care for this mangled crippled body?

And her face. You would have thought – locked into a grimace of pain, intense emotion. But no – her face on top of that crunched-up body her face was as absent as it had ever been. And if I could have drilled into her skull – or ripped it off – just to know what thoughts and feelings went through her head, then I would. I swear to God, I would.

There's a little stream of piss comes out of her now – green from all the wine. And it's the – funny to think of it now – it's the piss that focuses our minds.

And we organise and we call and we open doors and we're – you go in the ambulance I'll follow in a –

Oh please take care of my friend. Please. The most awful accident. Please.

As in that room she's wired up and dripped up and hooked up and we come and go and bring each other coffee and cigarettes and we pace the corridors and we ask the doctors and the nurses for news news news any news? We would never dare tell each other just how – and this is the word – exciting this is.

Did you feel that—? I wish there was something else but there was—

The excitement that all of us deny. Because excitement is not – no, not an appropriate response.

"It's touch and go with your friend," the doctor tells us. "It's distinctly touch and go."

Come on you cunt feel oh feel oh – but we look – we look like we're supposed to look, we do the – the little tilt of the head, the little sigh, the tear comes down the cheek – just like we know it should.

Her body – her body is broken in our head. A picture but not – it's not a feeling you know? And you would have thought above all else an artist would—

And in the room one of us or all of us – anyway somebody says to her:

"You can't hear but I have felt the most awful things towards you. And that won't continue. It can't continue. You are down and I am going to care for you. Please let me in and I will love you. Don't be absent. Be here. Please."

And back in her house we lay our heads down and we see them parading through our room – Sally with her breast eaten away, Ray with a lung no bigger than a matchbox and now this – and we want to join the parade and march down to hell or heaven or purgatory but we don't because

we have a diazepam and a smoke, a wine and a diazepam –
and that's okay.

The next day the personal trainer sobs. The cook howls. The
pool boy threatens an overdose. The boy who drained the
pool without notice the boy who – We console them. We
are all benificence. We discover – oh wonderful – what
good people we are.

And of course as soon as we humanly can we go to the
hospital.

We can't remember now. It doesn't matter. Oh of course
it matters to curators it matters to historians. But to us it
doesn't matter at all. But one of us first thought of taking
a camera.

We don't even know who first packed the digi-digi-digi-
digi-cam for our visit. Maybe we all did.

But there we are – hospital with the camera in our hand.

And we're here. We're here. We're here in the room with
the camera and the sunlight coming through the blinds.

Hello. Hello. It's us.

Please wake and stop us. Don't let us do that. You don't
have to burble on. Just open your eyes. That's all. Do you
know how much we used to – you were just so much a part
of us and now...

And we hold the camera down by our sides.

Come on. Just look. And see. And feel. And care. It's a
natural human thing. But we...

And you see now – look – what it's done to her. Now the
blood's been cleaned away. The body bruised and swollen into
shape no other human's yet achieved. Her limbs in plastic.
Her neck in plastic. Her mask. The drips and the tubes.
And the machines that inhalate and beeeep. A moving...a
timeless picture of the...

Our friend yes but also...

The line of the machine...

The purple of the bruise...

It appeals. It tempts. There is beauty here. We know, we've spent our life hunting it out and there is beauty here.

And we stand and we look and at last we're moved by the intense beauty of that image.

Throw camera – disgusting thing – through window and eight floors to the street below.

If you'd been in that room with us then maybe, maybe you'd have felt the same. Because today we are all artists.

And the light was good and the potential for composition was all there – and to be honest it was easy easy easy easy to come up with those images that so later seemed striking.

Stamp on that lens and shit on that viewfinder and tear the memory out by the soul.

And the temptation to arrange – just to move the bed...so... so the composition was...get her head in the light, so. The temptation was great and we were weak. So we wheel her into light and actually move the limbs and head – checking of course not to disrupt the tubes and drips and...science and Art can work together happily.

It took a few moments to snap. An image a record a frame.

Later, we sat in the smoking room and said to ourselves:

"That wasn't a good thing to do. That was a terrible thing to do. Why not select delete and wipe away what you've...? Why not?"

And we did. No – honest with you – we nearly did. But we never did.

And that night on the laptop we survey our work and we – ah – we are not disgusted with ourselves as we expect we should be. We are already thinking interviews – exhibition – catalogue – sale.

The next two months. The daily round.

The morning to the hospital wait for your chance collect your images while you can.

Oh how well we get to know that hospital! And for a while I actually dated the nurse – Miguel – we had blood tests to check for infections and confided the results but I wasn't ready to commit so that ended. And I think Miguel might actually have suspected – there were some questions – about the daily photos. Not that there was anything wrong...

Still we were furtive for that whole time. Maybe just for the thrill...

Then evenings back to survey what we've done.

Start to arrange, start to order, start to catalogue. Start to – print with a quality of drenched colour, tone and definition and...

Her home is our home, our studio. And in the morning the sun rises on us and at nights the sprinklers bless the lawn and we are fed and attended to by her staff.

And my body – during that time my body starts to rise and tauten as the trainer comes at six and we run through the suburbs to that gym and in the afternoon I swim fifty lengths in the pool.

I wish I'd had a nutritionist before. I feel fabulous.

And in time – the right dealer, the right agent, the right publicist – this will be an important series of images.

We've become fascinated by the – look you can see – fascinated by the way the markings and the bruisings and the cuts progress from day to day.

Just look. Just look. Just look and see. Isn't that rather interesting? Isn't that fascinating?

The way the bruises and the swellings grow and ripen over her. The myriad colours that a bruise can take. One day an eye revealed and then another concealed beneath the swollen. Yes.

And we feel together. We feel as one. There is a job of work to do and we are doing it.

Oh we are alive – would you look at that, the old corpse is back from the brink – and I'm shaking a stump and I'm walking the earth and I'm breathing the air.

Hurrah! Hurrah! Hurrah!

Don't sing it too loud but

Hurrah! Hurrah! Hurrah!

Join me if you will

Hurrah! Hurrah! Hurrah!

We're the Group! We're the Group! We're the Group!

But happiness is...happiness is so fast. Eight weeks and then...

We arrive as usual. And Miguel – we weren't dating by now that had finished some ooo – Miguel comes forward and he is smiling at us. Beaming.

And we know, we know. We can say the words for him.

"Your friend is conscious."

Oh.

Two months and Sleeping Beauty is...

Oh.

And I felt light because...because that had been...what was that—? Taking those images? Snatching that...? No no no no. That wasn't a thing that we were supposed to do. That was a...oh relief relief. This is...saved. I am so happy that Art has gone away and now we can be people.

That is wonderful.

Let her be present. Please. Let her be...

I did a line before I went into her room. I never told anybody that before. I knew I had just enough for a line and in the nappy-changing facility I... I don't understand myself.

"Hello. Look it's us. We're all here."

She's not awake – not awake like you and me – she's slipping in and out – but sometimes her eyes open and she'll look at us and she sees us. She's in the room with us. Once she even gives us her smile. I swear to God.

And we're happy. For her. But also for us. A quiet happy but still...

And we talk that hospital talk that burble that you talk to the semi-conscious and to babies. We burble a nice sound because she deserves the sweetest baby talk.

"We're going to go skinny-dipping. Any day now. That's what we're gonna do. We're gonna get you out of here. And we're all gonna strip and it's going to be back...

...You will be one of us just as it was all the decade past everything stripped away and us just a bunch of cunts of dicks and titties and bumcracks us the bathing beautiful oh think of that my darling think of. We are so lucky to have known and we'll know it again. We will. We will. We will."

I kiss her. She doesn't do anything. But that's okay. Everything is...

And we say to each other: It's over. She's mending. Happy days are coming.

And we hold hands and we smile and we hug and we sing. The Group stand around her bed and we sing and she opens her eyes and she looks at us and...

I think for a moment...no.

Yes I thought... I don't know whether anyone else thought...

Maybe all of us thought...

She knows. She knows what we have been doing. She sees the camera in our pocket and she understands. How much wiser than us she is.

But that couldn't be.

So we hold the water to her lips and we stroke her fingers and we breathe:

"We love you."

And she says:

"Thank you for being my friends through all of these years."

And – no – she didn't know that thoughts of hate had ever gone through our heads and we are – well – blessed – and – um – absolved by those words. And that feels very good.

And for hours we are there with her as she sleeps and wakes and I think this was the...calmest I have ever been in my life.

So why – back at her house did we start to—? I let the gym slip those weeks. My belly sags.

I drive-thru and the chicken wings and ice cream until my stomach burns.

One night with lots of wine and spliff and cokeycokeycoke an actual row. Subject – nothing. But screaming and slamming and tears and silence.

And actually you know it's at moments like this that I find that my depepependcy issues really emerge? Because I want to – oh Counsellor – I want to be part of the Group that's what I want so much but if they won't maybe I've excluded mmmm ah shit there's no fucking needles in this fucking room what's a hospital room without a needle you know?

And the – I'll give you a hundred to sleep with me. Leave the pool for a moment. Leave the pool alone just for one goddam minute and give me one good fuck won't you? What is wrong with my money?

And Ray and Tommy and Sally are rattling around in my room. Call it a drug-abuse-related issue if you like. But I call it grief when the bones of dead friends are banging against your head and drowning out the sounds of life, while we... Eat. Sleep. Shit. Wank. Begin again. Eat. Sleep. Shit. Wank. Begin again.

Oh yes. That's right. One of us decided to show her the images. Well – I can't remember which...

I don't think it was me but...

Maybe I could have...

Anyway one of us – we were – what? – all in the room and there was something about her smile then, the way she looked at us as we cared for her.

I felt like she was accusing me and I...

It's so hard to know what she's thinking. Always been like that. But normally you feel like she's...judging.

And I just wanted...

Somebody thought: I have to tell her. To make myself feel better.

Maybe to hurt her.

And she was looking down at her body – still purple and twisted – and she says:

"No mirror anywhere. I must look like shit. I guess they don't want me to see what..."

And there was a voice:

"Oh you can see what you look like."

"Yes?"

"But maybe you shouldn't. Maybe it's best."

"No. I'd like to see."

She didn't stop us you see, there was every chance.

"You've got a mirror?"

"No but..."

The laptop out. That first week in the hospital. She's barely human. Scroll. Week two, three, on through the months. She begins to heal.

And she's watching. But I couldn't see...

Still nothing in her eyes.

And then she asks:

"Where do these come from?"

And so we: We took them.

And I thought she'd understand the evil inside us. But I really don't think she did because anyway she says:

"Thank you." Like she means it.

She didn't want us to put the laptop away. But we did. The battery was running flat.

And then she says:

"Can you take me to the toilet?"

They'd removed her catheter by then and so I supported her to the toilet and I felt okay because I was holding her and she really needed me.

And you know there were visits when she didn't mention the images. I don't know – three? four? – several visits when they didn't come up.

In my mind several weeks when they were unspoken. And I suppose actually it wasn't wrong, it was – what's the word? – kind to record that for her.

Well yes, if we'd done it for her. Yes. And if we hadn't arranged the body. Planned the exhibition. If we could forget.

And then one day she says:

"Bring the camera."

"Oh...no."

"Yes. Bring the camera. I want to carry on. I'm still healing. I'm getting stronger all the time. And I'd like to carry on recording that."

What could we do but bring the camera?

She laughed that day. She was so happy. She turned her head into the light to show the bruise. She pulled up the gown to show the wounds, the stitches, the bone almost sticking through the blue flesh.

She is driven by an energy we haven't seen for years.

"You stand over there. Here – get the drip in the frame beside the cuts on the hand."

And we carry out her commands. So many images and then:

"Let me see let me see let me see myself."

It's an order. Delivered like a child but still...

And so we scroll through and she studies intently and oh...

That's the kind of moment when any sane person needs a K hole you know? Just to get you out of that room.

And she likes them.

And all that energy.

Every day she drives us on. And every day is recording her.

The old routine was naughty. She was sleeping. We were snatching bits of her. And now...

It is our job to make her happy. And she loves this. And she grows stronger every day. While we...we actually started to feel rather sickly you know?

I have headaches. I have migraines. This morning I slipped while shaving and see the see the cut. No it's alright but yes yes actually it does actually sting. But you mustn't worry about me. Doctor doctor I think the pool boy may have passed on something fungal. I'm yeasty and I want to cry about it.

We want her to sleep. We don't want her to tire herself. She should be sleeping all the time but now...we are the exhausted ones. The visits to the hospital. The fluorescent light. That bad coffee. It is very tiring.

And now she wants hard copies. So we provide hard copies.

And she lays them out around the room, arranges, rearranges, studies. And – yes – sometimes she does ask our opinions but really it is her eye, her eye shaping them into a form.

She is so good at what she does. She has shown at such fantastic galleries. You actually learn from her working her way through those images. Which is a privilege.

But we still have to take her to the toilet. Remember. At the end of the day...we still have to take her to the toilet.

It had never crossed our mind that she might have other visitors so when we saw...

Tall. Rich. Tanned. Bit of a cunt.

"Who was he?"

"He owns the gallery that I work with out here. We've been talking about the work I want to show when I get out of here."

What work?

"Oh...just ideas."

But I knew. It was lost then. It was her body. She had dived into the pool. It was her act. And we thought we took the images but she was the work. And she has everything and we have – oh – nothing.

I can't do this any fucking longer you know? Give me a break. Let me succeed.

She would claim the images and we would be back in the bohemian quarter doing – oh – very good work with the underprivileged. But be honest – I've done my dues – I want to be privileged.

And now it feels like punishment to take those daily images of her. You can hear what will be said about her. You know who will buy these.

I must do something else with my life. But what?

So have a party in her room. Spliffaway. Let's feel as though we're all together in this and making these pictures. Let's really do everything we can to feel that.

And now the time comes. It's winter. She's coming home.

Excitement. Something we can organise.

She's made a list of course. Clothes and make-up that we have to take to prepare her. In we go. She's sitting on the bed, expectant, ready now to go. Clothes on with some assistance, make-up artfully applied.

And walking through the ward she looks so strong so well. Amongst the injured dying lines she looks so strong as if to insult each of them one by one. And it's us following behind who look the weaker. The weak ones stepping in her step.

But on the street – where the healthy ones parade around and flirt and deal and hustle and threaten – well there – even as she passes through the revolving door and into the rain – suddenly she seems the weaker. Suddenly you see the way her limbs are now not set quite right, the drag and hobble of her frame. You see the way no make-up known can quite conceal the swollen face. Just one step from hospital to street – but all the difference. And she's the stranger here. This is our world – despite the shabby little lives we've led – this is our world and she's not quite finding her feet.

And we are good again. We are good. As we help her into the taxi, give directions, hold her as a bump or turn inflicts a little pain upon her. We're here for you, we're guiding you, we love you. We're taking you through the darkness. Trust us. Love us. Please.

She's tired at home. She takes in banners cakes the pool. A little smile – that little smile she's always given year on year and never given anything away. The smile that you can make of what you will. But the smile done she's dozing and we say:

"Come on to bed to bed to rest that's what you need it's all so much you need to rest."

And we watch over her and we do care for her. We do genuinely – it's very important that you should believe this bit – we do genuinely care.

There's interrupted sleep. She's seeing it again and again when her eyes are shut. Slipping off the clothes. The leap into the air. The arc up and up into the stars. Swoop down. And then the instant of concrete. The instant of knowledge of all the pain that must come and then – crack. And she's awake.

But we're there. There's always one of us there. And she smiles and says

"Thank you thank you thank you thank you for being here."

And we say:

"Silly you silly no we want to be here."

And it's true. We do. We really do.

And she has visitors. Her manager. Her publicist. The gallery owner.

And we welcome them and we show them up to her room.

And we smile at them and offer them drinks and we can't make out the words of the conversation that is going on above our heads.

But really we know. We know that this story. Her story. The pictures. This is what they are dealing in. Selling. Packaging. Promoting. Launching. They are getting ready for the launch day.

And we are housemaids really and any day now we'll be deported home.

And look honestly years ago who would have thought...? She was the least of us honestly.

Then one day she

"Let's get out the images. Let's put them out around the room."

Here we go. Here we go. She's preparing. So we...

No no you're not ready you're not ready for that not while you're getting better no not now later we can go through them.

Promise?

Of course of course we promise you.

And that was meant. We meant it then. Nothing hidden then.

I wouldn't say the virus was willed. It wasn't quite as clear as that. No one of us actually sat down and said

"Come you virus come enter in my inbox spread your stain through modem into memory and mainframe come."

That would be ridiculous. But I do think one of us in our heart of wretched hearts knew that the attachment was a dupe, knew that opening "read me" would wreck the laptop file by file, taking out the images – zap zappy zappy zap.

We protested

Shit shit shit

But we hadn't backed up so...something going on more than just a freak.

Didn't tell her. Kept on

Rest now and when you're then the images yes yes yes.

And we hadn't lost them all. The bulk had but there were some still in the camera memory, a few hard copies left. Enough to piece together even if – even if – even if –

Well even if chunks of – great big chunks of actually – whole chapters of – some key bits of the – even if "read me" had actually fucked up the story of her healing so now she healed in leaps and starts – a nonsense narrative.

But there was a kind of – still enough to satisfy her need no doubt.

And the day was coming. The day was coming now. The day when we had promised her that she could see the images laid out from the first stolen shots of her swollen mangled totally unconscious frame right through to those final few days – the final rush of wellness in the hospital.

Tomorrow we tell her tomorrow. Tomorrow you will come down and it will all be presented in the living room – the gallery of you.

Thank you

She says and off she drifts sleeping with the calmest smile you've ever seen.

And we sit in silence. Waiting for...

Oh God.

Waiting for...

I blame the personal trainer. He wouldn't be the first – is there a personal trainer in this world who doesn't deal as well as train? But it was the personal trainer who dealt us the stuff that night. He was selling but yes okay and we were buying.

I thought I was clean I really thought I was so clean. But I'm not. I never am. Never will be. I'm a user and I always will be. Until the day I die. Isn't that great? Isn't it fucking great? Because I know who I am. This is me. I'm a userjunkiecuntcrackwhorefeelmyKholecuntedtwat that's me and it feels...fucking great.

I am alive I am alive. Sober is dead. The faces of the fucking sober dead and I am so fucking from my cunt to my arse to my tits to my mouth I am fucking alive.

Kiss me kiss me somebody stick a tongue in me or up me or I don't fucking care come on humans let's human each other or sniff cracks I don't care let's be human isn't that great with the this is are you up? I'm up and up and up and up and cunted and cunted and c-c-c-c-cunted. Woah! There's no fucking coming down now.

Turn the music up turn the music up turn the music up turn the music up I want my stomach to bleeeeeeeeeed when you turn the music up.

And then one of us produced the camera, produced the memory. Choose our first image and

Delete

Oh yes oh yes oh yes oh yes oh yes.

And then a great wave of fun

Select Delete Select Delete Select Delete Select Delete
Select Delete Select Delete Select Delete Select Delete
Select Delete Select Delete Select Delete Select Delete
Select Delete Select Delete Select Delete Select Delete
Select Delete Select Delete Select Delete Select Delete
Select Delete Select Delete Select Delete Select Delete
Select Delete Select Delete Select Delete Select Delete
Select Delete Select Delete Select Delete Select Delete
Select Delete Select Delete Select Delete Select Delete
Select Delete Select Delete Select Delete Select Delete

Select Delete Select Delete Select Delete Select Delete
Select Delete Select Delete Select Delete Select Delete

Until not a single memory of the "miracle of healing" left.

A little pause then as we drunk in what we'd done. A little
chance to celebrate how strong we are now. God – the
triumph pumping through our torsos.

But look...there's the hard copies. Yes the hard copies. The
last remaining bit.

Let's stop now. It's done now. We know we are strong. We
know it.

I'm coming down. Look at me. I'm coming down actually.
Fuck I need water.

Oh no we're up now. Please let's...please don't let this end.

This is the only thing we will ever do on this planet and
we know that. Our lives are nothing. Our work is nothing.
No be honest with ourselves fucksake our work is nothing.

And our work is nothing and we are no people. We have
ruined our lives. We took a wrong turning into art and it has
taken us nowhere and it's too late now to discover our talent.

And look at our bodies look at them my tits are jjjjjjust
moving every day towards the grave.

And I wish I had Aids or cancer – Sally lucky Ray lucky – Aids
or cancer so I didn't have to suffer the slow drip-drip-drip-
indignity of the everyday drag of life.

So – don't turn back now. Don't do that.

Pedro – come back over here and bring as much fucking
gear as you've got we'll buy the lot.

Alright my friends alright. This is it. Music please from
every speaker. Stick a bit of porn on the plasma and it's...
chemical roulette...whatever you pull out the hat you inject
or inhale or you stuff up your arse.

Here we go here here we go here h – h-h-h-h-h-h – here
weeee g-g – g-gooooo!

And the lighter – the first flame on the corner of the first image of her healing. We whoop and laugh and are delighted at the flames flaring up and blanking it away.

Taking it in turns now

Let me burn I'm next I'm the next to burn

The bonfire

And we dance we dance about in total free free freedom as the images away in guttering and fumes and blaze.

It's going it's going it's going soon be nothing left.

What's going on?

She's there. Just a T-shirt and she's in the doorway.

What are you doing?

And we want to say:

"You know you know you know what we're doing. Surely you know you knew we had to?"

But we don't. We stand and watch her. Silence. She's moving in. She takes the centre. And she takes it in. And sees.

And she understands then – she knows.

Everything she thought was friendship was hate. Everything that was care was envy. Concern was destroy. And we hold her in her hands and we have snapped her neck and we have broken her legs and we have trodden on her skull.

And finally. Oh finally she is absent no longer. She is totally... there. And her eyes take us in. And it's as if we can hear her say – her mouth is closed, but still I, we, I we, heard:

"You are small people. You have always been small people. Ever since the day. There are small people and there are big people. And I am a big person and you are not. Yes? Yes? Yes?

"Oh I've held this in all these years but no more.

"I have talent. I have vision. I am blessed.

"None of you can ever touch me.

"You thought I didn't see all your jealousy and hatred all these years? Of course I saw it.

"And Sally and Ray died because they were too weak to live, to live and and make art.

"I am the only one of you strong enough ever to really live and nothing you can do will ever destroy me. Because I will always be the stronger.

"So write to me please from time to time and let me know about your small lives."

And you know when she said it – such a relief that she wasn't absent any more after so many years.

And really – oh really – it was.

And so really I suppose it was one of the happiest nights of my life.

No actually it was the happiest night of my life. To have somebody tell you the truth like that...try to get somebody to do it to you if you can...try it tonight...it's really fantastic.

And now. Years have gone. And look at these arms – no track marks – nothing. Clean. And these four here – new teeth. Beauties.

And I actually met someone who I rather like and I have two children – one is two, the other is four – and they like me so that makes it feel rather better. Because when we're all playing around the paddling pool things seem rather okay. And the children have their own little mobile phones – for safety – and they like to take pictures of Mummy lying in the pool. And that's lovely.

And I like to think there's a rehab or an Aids ward or a somewhere where we'll be together once again. Somewhere where we'll meet and be the gang. But – hey I'm a romantic. I'm a foolish old romantic as the years go on.

So. Light the candles. Bake the cake. Sing the song. The gang's all here. We're here together. And the dream is dreamy and oh life is long.

VISIT THE SAMUEL FRENCH BOOKSHOP AT THE ROYAL COURT THEATRE

Browse plays and theatre books, get expert advice and enjoy a coffee

Samuel French Bookshop
Royal Court Theatre
Sloane Square
London
SW1W 8AS
020 7565 5024

Shop from thousands of titles on our website

 samuelfrench.co.uk

 samuelfrenchltd

 samuel french uk

Lightning Source UK Ltd.
Milton Keynes UK
UKHW020642200621
385824UK00005B/108